Y0-BZX-127

Suzhou-The City of Charm

名 城 苏 州

中国民族摄影艺术出版社

Experience the Old City Of Suzhou

Suzhou has been known as Wu for 2500 years.

It was first built as the capital of the Wu kingdom during the reign of King He-lü. Until today,the suburb of the city is still called the County of Wu. Refined over time, the local dialect is well known throughout the country as the Soft Tones of Wu.

The hieroglyph of the word"Wu", as well as its pronunciation in the dialect today, can trace their origins to the word"fish",which has been abundant in the waters of Wu. Since the distant past, its numerous canals have channeled every corner of the city. The lives and the destiny of its people have always been intertwined with the surrounding waters.

The streets and canals in the city form a unique layout that resembles overlaid rectangular grids. These canals are evidence of the continuous effort to tame and comb the regional waterways throughout history. Well-preserved neighborhoods can still be found in the northeast district of the city, as well as the ancient towns of Lu-zhi, Zhou-zhuang, and Tong-li, to the southeast of Suzhou.

These illustrate a timeless scene where the trickling water is the lifeblood of the town, where the stone staircases and the arching bridges bear witness to the ever-changing lives inside the white-washed walls alongside the canals. For the residents here, the boat is their main transportation. The housewives left their marks on the stone staircases leading to the water, where generation after generation cleaned rice and did laundry. The life here is as quaint and peaceful as the water surrounding it. Who would have thought, even as the venerable minister Wu Zixu who deliberated over the design of this great capital and the life in it, that these canals would inspire so many poets over centuries to celebrate the classic realm henceforth described as"arching bridges, trickling water, and exquisite dwellings?"Who

could have predicted, as residents of today's metropolis enjoy their newfound prosperity, that in this very place one may still realize the dream that was China?

That poetic, and sometimes mysterious, tranquility of the city life here often brings about the contemplation of her past. One doesn't have to go far, though, to touch that past. Just enter through any tall, wood-paneled gate, and you'll find another microcosm, in which there is an exquisite courtyard in every household, a garden everywhere you turn to.

During the Ming dynasty, there were 271 gardens in record, of which more than sixty still survive. The largest one, the Humble Administrator's Garden, has over five acres. The smallest, the Grainy Remnant Garden, has only 146 square meters.

In the comfort of his home, the owner would realize his own dreams with landscape that is often comprised of ponds readily dug on the ground and mounds stacked with rocks from distant mountains. Kiosks, terraces, pavilions, among many different types of dwellings, would find their way to the top of the mounds or the edge of the ponds. These are chic spots where one may visit to observe the change of seasons, to listen to the rain falling on the leaves, to smell the aroma of the new blossom, to play music, and to receive the teachings of the ancients. The inscriptions on these structures are not only to show off the scholarship of the owner, but also to convey their true beliefs. The same philosophy can be found in the placement of the plants and the collection of exotic rocks in the garden. These items are often personified to convey symbolic meanings and to express emotions.

The physical components of a Suzhou garden are landscape, plants and architecture. A garden is an art piece emphasizing its intricate scenery, without losing its livability. Over time, the garden has emerged as a product and carrier as well of all the personal interests, emotions, and sentiments of the Chinese scholars. To understand it is to observe it in silence, and to enjoy it as a place for meditation and inward inspection. It is only then that you will find that written all over it is an epic of the evolution of Chinese philosophy and scholarship.

Suzhou gardens were homes of retired high officials and prominent local families. Evidences of such abound in the design and construction of these gardens.

A garden, first of all ,must be small and compact. A small environment brings coziness, where the harmony among man, architecture and nature is manifest. Compactness also implies exquisiteness, where nature, culture, space and time are all effectively represented in one small place.

It must also remain simple and low-key, a quality that is prerequisite for harmony. For those who have retired from public life, what's the point of excess extravagance? Life after an illustrious career can only be satisfied by the basic shades of black and white. Plants and rocks are merely paintings on the canvas made of the white walls. The permanence of space and time is ingeniously captured in the dynamic balance between Black and White.

It must appear natural. Otherwise there can be no beauty. The art of forming rocks with the complement of water, as well as the engineering ingenuity in the architecture of bridges and houses, are so sophisticated that the whole arrangement comes forward unpretentiously, "as if crafted by God". Winding trails always blend into the ground. Curling branches on old trees grow mottled over time. All is the work of nature. For one to pace inside the garden is to enjoy, with humility, the togetherness with nature.

The gardens are to be visited with a peace of mind. The landscape and architecture have to be experienced from an ordinary person's point of view. There is no need for the feeling of awe usually associated with pilgrimages to palaces, nor should one anticipate mysterious wonders at the end of every exploration.

The gardens are to be visited with a "third eye", like that of an experienced photographer. A garden is not only about the elements that are physically present, but also about the light and shadow, the reflection in the water, etc. These are vital components, physical and virtual, of the beauty that makes Suzhou gardens unique, along with windows that are always strategically placed to double-function as picture frames for the scenery.

The gardens are to be visited with the understanding that the water and the rocks form a dynamic partnership of change and permanence. They bring on the state of mind that is best described by the well-known poem "the forest only quieter when the cicadas chirp, the mountain much more serene when the birds sing". Here, in the midst of a metropolis, one comes to seek the spiritual transcendence where "the mind is still, the body no longer distinguishable, both in harmony with the universe".

The Suzhou gardens, as well as the Soft Tones of Wu, the local forms of vocal art Ping Tan or Kun Opera, from which the Peking Opera traces its roots, are the most vital experiences preserved from a culture of 2500 years. Anybody, so long as he knows a little about history, a little about the Yangtze delta, will no doubt gasp, upon opening this album, "Oh! Suzhou!"

Suzhou has been known as Wu for 2500 years. This is a unique place and you won't find another one like this anywhere else.

Xiao Lei
6/01/2001

读古城苏州

苏州即吴。

两千五百年前吴王阖闾在此始建大城。今天，苏州城周地域叫吴县，苏州话被称为吴侬软语，而"吴"字的书写起源以及直到今天吴地方言的发音，都与"鱼"相似相同。所以，显而易见，自古以来苏州城里城外，由水沟通着；苏州人家房前屋后，被鱼儿簇拥着。

苏州城在治水、理水的历史进程中，形成了独特的水陆双棋盘格局。至今保留完好的苏州古城东北一隅和城东南古镇角直、周庄、同里便是成片的以缓缓流水为命脉，高低错落的粉墙黑瓦为依傍，拱桥、石阶沟通其间的水乡景观。傍水而居的水乡人，船便是他们主要的交通工具。屋前的石阶，镌刻着家庭主妇淘米洗衣的生活足迹。苏州人的生活节奏，和门前的水一样平缓舒缓。她的奠基人吴国大臣伍子胥无论如何也不会想到，以人类生活为目的的河道体系会成为千百年来文人咏唱的"小桥、流水、人家"的诗的意境，会成为经济发达年代都市人寻找中国梦的地方。

如诗如梦，是因为她的幽静。静以致远，让人遥想她的过去。其实不必遥想，只须走进高高的墙门，就会发现另一个世界，那便是苏州人世代居住的地方：家家庭院、处处园林。

明朝年间，苏州已有园林二百七十一个，几经沧桑，至今仍有大小园林庭院六十余处。最大的园林拙政园占地五公顷之多，最小的庭院残粒园仅一百四十六平方米。园主或移来远处的山石，或就地挖池叠山，在自己的家中营造了有山有水的小天地。于是，观景的、听雨的、闻香的、操琴的、读经的各类建筑亭、台、楼、阁、轩在山上、在池边应景而生。建筑上的匾额、对联既让文人小露才气，更是他们直抒胸臆的载体。于是，园林内遍植的梅兰竹菊、园内收藏的湖石、书条石都为之赋予了普遍的人格意义，带上了园主鲜明的情感色彩。

从苏州园林的外在形式看，是人工营造的山水、花草和建筑，所以它可看、可游、可居；从苏州园林形成的历史及原因看，是中国文人所有情趣、情感、情操的物化和寄托，所以它宜静观、静思，从中读出个中国文人的思想史来。

苏州园林庭院是苏州退隐官宦和殷实人家的住处，因此带有明显的居所特征。首先它小巧，因为小巧，所以温馨，人在其中感受到与自然、与建筑的充分和谐；因为小巧，必定精致，在不大的空间浓缩了自然，浓缩了时空，浓缩了文化。其次它素朴，因为素朴，所以和谐，既退隐江湖，何必显耀张扬，在经历了华丽辉煌之后，回归到黑与白的原始极色，粉墙为纸，花石为绘，在黑白的变化对比中，捕捉永恒。其三它自然，因为自然，所以美丽，叠山理水、架桥构屋，处处匠心，却表现为不经意之作，"宛如天开"。小径曲曲弯弯，与路边泥土浑然一体，老树虬枝斑斑驳驳，尽展自然本色，人行其中，只有与自然共处的愉悦，绝无征服自然的霸气。

游苏州园林，要有一颗平常心，以一个普通人身居其中的感觉来感受山水楼台，既不必怀朝拜宫阙的虔诚，也不必有寻幽探秘的期盼。游苏州园林，要善用摄影家的"第三只眼睛"。因为除了园林实景之外，还有它的光影、树影、水中倒影构成虚实交错的美，以及各种窗景、框景组成的画面美。游苏州园林，既要有"动观流水静观山"的眼光，又要有"蝉噪林愈静，鸟鸣山更幽"的心境，以求"心凝形释，与万物冥合"的升华。

苏州园林和评弹、昆曲、吴侬软语是二千五百年苏州留存至今的最鲜活的感受。任何人，如果他稍稍了解一点历史，稍稍知道一点江南，只要打开画册，就一定会叫起来：哦，苏州！

苏州即吴。苏州是独一无二，无可取代的。

肖 雷

2001年1月6日

A Canal in the Old City

古城水巷

The Master-of -Nets Garden

园林 网师园

The Ancient Towns

古

镇

The Taihu Lake

太湖

The Tiger Hill

虎

丘

The Classical Gardens
World Cultural Heritage

古典园林 世界文化遗产

拙政园晨雾
The Humble Administrator's Garden in Morning Mist

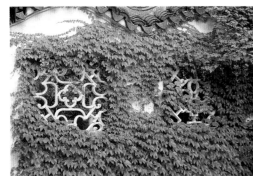

花　窗
Latticed Window

见山楼
The Mountain-in-View Tower

荷风四面亭
The Pavilion in Lotus Breeze

待霜亭红叶
The Orange Pavilion

临水长廊
The Waterside Corridor

砖雕门楼
Carved Brick Gateway

万卷堂
The Hall of Ten-Thousand Books

远借北寺塔
Pagoda in Distance

网师园雪景
Snow Scene in the Master-of
-Nets Garden

月到风来亭
The Moon and
Breeze Pavilion

园林小品
Small ornaments in the Gardens

花　窗
Latticed Window

留园雪景
Snow Scene in the Lingering Garden

冠云峰
Cloud Crowned Peak

留园厅堂
Halls in the Lingering Garden

五峰仙馆
The Celestial Hall of Five Peaks

可亭、紫藤
The Passable Pavilion,
Purple Wisteria

环秀山庄
The Mountain Villa in Secluded Beauty

狮子林
The Lion Grove Garden

"涉趣"洞门
The Entrance Gate of "Stepping
into the World of Interests"

"燕誉堂"
The Hall of Swallow's Blessing

雾中假山

Garden Hills in Mist

怡 园
The Garden of Harmony

沧浪亭
The Surging Wave Garden

耦 园
The Couple's Garden

艺 圃
The Garden of Cultivation

园林小品
Small ornaments in the
Gardens

退思园

The Garden of Retreat and Reflection

The Ancient City

千年古城

水巷隆冬
The Canal in Winter

古运河之春
The Ancient Canal in Spring

虎丘远眺
The Tiger Hill Viewed From Distance

吴中第一名胜——虎丘
The Top Historical Monument of Wu Region-Tiger Hill

水巷夕照
A Canal in Evening Glow

吴门古桥
Ancient Bridge in Wumen Gate

双 塔
The Twin Pagoda

报恩寺塔
Bao En Temple Pagoda

宝带桥
The Precious Belt Bridge

枕河人家
Houses Hanging Over Canals

枫桥铁岭关
The Iron Bell Fortress on Maple Bridge

佛 事
Buddhism Ceremony

济公罗汉
Monk named Ji Gong

寒山、拾得罗汉
Twin Statues of Han Shan and Shi De, Two Master Monks

寒山寺
The Hanshan Temple

枕河人家
Houses Hanging Over Canals

普明宝塔

The Hanshan Temple Pagoda

昆　曲
Kun Opera

Ancient Water Towns

水乡古镇

双 桥
The Twin Bridge

田 野
Farming Fields

采红菱　Harvesting Water Nuts

洗 菜　Rinsing Vegetables

水乡春雨
Spring Drizzling in Countryside

水巷悠悠
Peaceful Canal

路边早市
Early Market by the Side of Streets

生活光影
Light of Life

自得其乐
Each Enjoys His Own

三 桥
Three Bridges

晨 院
Courtyard in the
Morning

夏日晚餐
Supper in Summer

水乡印象
Impressions of the Countryside

唠家常
Small Talks

水乡婚礼
Wedding Ceremony in
the Countryside

农家日行早
Start Early for Farming

夕 归

Homebound in Sunset

古镇之夜
Night View of an Ancient Town

水乡似仙境

The Appealing Scenery of Countryside

A Scene of Taihu Lake

太湖风光

太湖春早
Early Spring of Taihu Lake

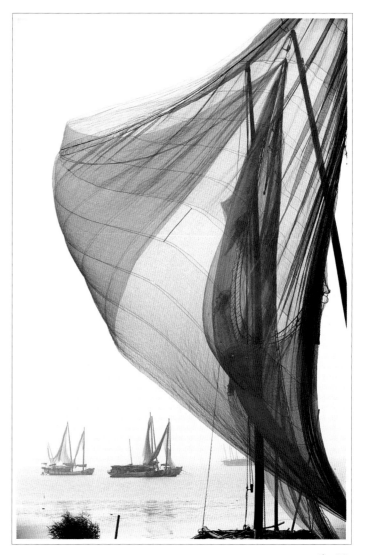

渔 汛
Fishing Season

天平山红枫
Red Maples in the
Tianping Hill

上方山
The Shanfang Hill·

1.光福古塔
An Ancient Pagoda in Guangfu Town

2."清、奇、古、怪"古松柏
Four Old Pine Trees, Each Named as
Uprightness, Remarkableness, Seniority
and Fantasy

3.灵岩山
The Divine Rock Hill

4.高义园
The Garden of Righteousness

日出满湖金
Lake Aglow With Rising Sun

湖畔小景
A Lakeside Scene

"香雪海"——梅花林
Plum Forest-A Sea of Fragrant Snow

上学路上
On Their Way to School

古桥、老树
Old Bridge, Old Tree

太湖大桥
The Taihu Bridge

鱼 塘　Fish Pond

渔 港　The Fish Dock

风来车转　Windmill

渔 港　The Fish Dock

归 舟
Returning Vessels

图书在版编目(CIP)数据

名城苏州/郑翔，夏至主编.－北京：中国民族摄影
艺术出版社，2001.5
ISBN 7-80069-363-5
Ⅰ.名… Ⅱ.①郑…②夏… Ⅲ.摄影集－苏州市
－当代 Ⅳ.J533
中国版本图书馆CIP数据核字(2001)第032293号

主　　编:郑　翔　夏　至
责任编辑:吕小中
文　　字:肖　雷
设　　计:吴　溶
翻　　译:朱骁洵　徐伟荣
电脑制作:翟爱英
摄　　影:郑　翔　印祖庆　刘智常　陶剑秋
　　　　　马景明　俞小康　任祝成　李　江

出版：中国民族摄影艺术出版社
承印：北京宏达恒智印艺有限公司
开本：850 × 1168mm　1/24
版次：2001年4月第一版第一次印刷
印张：3.75　　(0006000)
书号：ISBN 7-80069-363-5/J·283

COUNTRY HEIGHTS
Even Something for Better living
绿野集团

打破传统的住家概念
迈向另一个崭新的家居环境

绿野运动休闲住宅

绿野集团欲在各主要省市寻求300-600华亩合适的土地，
打造一项与世界连线的绿野运动休闲住宅计划，并在全国建立起3000个以上的
羽球场、篮球场以及游泳池，使居住者能够拥有优美的家居环境，
同时享受运动与休闲的便利。

—中国国际航空股份有限公司

务世界

北京2008年奥运会航空客运合作伙伴
AIRLINE PARTNER OF THE BEIJING 2008 OLYMPIC GAMES

免费垂询电话　800-810-1111